Playhouse Creatures

A play

April De Angelis

Samuel French — London
New York - Toronto - Hollywood

PLAYHOUSE CREATURES

Commissioned and first performed by The Sphinx—
Women's National Touring Theatre—on 5th October
1993, at the Haymarket Theatre Studio in Leicester, with
the following cast:

Doll Common	Jean Marlow
Nell Gwyn	Fleur Bennett
Mrs Farley	Nicola Grier
Mrs Betterton	Frances Cuka
Mrs Marshall	Geraldine Fitzgerald

Directed by Sue Parrish
Designed by Annabel Lee
Lighting by Di Stedman
Music by Claire van Kampen

The play is set in London

Time: approximately 1670

COPYRIGHT INFORMATION

(See also page ii)

For Holly

The first production of this play was dedicated to
Elizabeth Howe whose book *The First English
Actresses* was a source of inspiration.

"That men of quality should take up with and spend
themselves and fortunes in keeping little playhouse
creatures, foh!"

Mrs Squeamish in *The Country Wife*
by William Wycherley

CHARACTERS

Doll Common, an old woman
Nell Gwyn, a sixteen-year-old girl
Mrs Betterton, an actress of fifty
Mrs Marshall, an actress in her late twenties
Mrs Farley, an actress in her early twenties

PROLOGUE

Doll Common enters. She is sixty or so. She seems a vagrant, timeless. She warms her hands at a small fire. She addresses the audience

Doll It is a fact that I was born. That is a fact. The how was in that old eternal way, but the when I shall not divulge. No, I'll keep that hugged close to my chest like a sick cat.

Pause

Once this was a playhouse, and before that, a bear pit. On a hot day, I swear you could still smell the bears. They used to rag me. "That ain't the bears, Doll, that's the gentlemen!" But it was bears because upon occasion as I swept I came upon their hair. Tufts of it bunched up in corners which I saved. As a small child, my father was the bear keeper. I remember the bears moaning at night, and licking the wounds at their throats where the irons cut in and sighing, for while bears love to dance they hate to do it for a whip. Indeed, under those conditions, I believed they preferred the fighting to the dancing, even as blood was spilt and death faced. Sometimes I still hear their cries, very faint and in the wind. (*She stops and listens*)

ACT I

Nell (*off*) Doll? Doll?

Nell Gwyn enters

Is that you, Doll? I'm cold. I swear I've never been so cold.

Doll laughs

It ain't funny, Doll. Let's have a bit of your fire. (*She muscles in*)
Doll You ain't changed.
Nell I fancy something. I fancy hot chocolate. Warm and frothy in a
silver cup.
Doll There ain't none here, your ladyship.
Nell I'll ring a bell.
Doll There ain't no bell.
Nell No bell? How d'you change the scenes then?
Doll You're slow, ain't you?

Nell looks about her

Nell This is an odd place.

Pause

It's dark. Dark and it stinks.

Pause. Nell gives a cry

Here, Doll. We're not, are we?

Doll laughs

No, Doll, No!
Doll (*mimicking*) Oh no, Doll, no.
Nell Aren't I at rest, then?

Doll begins to recite, as a taunt, a reminder

Doll   "Our play we perform for you this night
                 For no greater cause than your delight"
Nell This is a dream. One where I forget me lines.
Doll   "We ask alone but one small favour
                 That you critics have some sweet flavour
                 'Cos heaven be praised tis not so wise an age
                 But that your own follies may supply the stage."
                 (*She does a little dance*)
Nell Stop it, Doll, stop it.

Doll laughs

We need a priest, Doll. A priest!

Doll rings a small bell she has about her

You had a bell, you bleedin' liar!
Doll A priest!

Doll exits

Nell runs after her and exits

SCENE 2

The whole atmosphere changes as Mrs Farley enters

The stage becomes light, resembling a summer's day on a London street

Mrs Farley speechifies in religious tones

Mrs Farley And lo
                It is written in our Lord's book

That this time shall come to pass.
And ye have only to look about ye and ye will see
that it has come to pass.
Yes, it hath.

Nell enters, as if from a pub doorway. She holds a jug

Nell (*calling in*) All right! All right! In a bleedin' minute! (*She sighs in exasperation and sits down*)

Mrs Farley Ye shall see that the cows do not give sweet milk
but are dry except for stinking curdles.
Ye shall find all men to be cheats and their hair
to be lice riddled.
Yeah, ye shall discover even the women at your hearth
to be fornicators!

Nell (*calling in once more*) I'm having a fucking break!

Mrs Farley And a great plague of locusts will settle in the fields and pester your cows... (*She starts to cry*)

Nell You crying? Don't take it personal. I always shout.

Mrs Farley Usually I take round the hat. Just then I was making it up. Could you tell?

Nell Seemed all right.

Mrs Farley He was my dad, the preacher. It was last rites all summer with the plague. He said God was protecting him. And then, just last week, when it seemed to be over, the boils came up. Purple. Behind his knees. This morning thought I better just carry on. You know. This was our spot.

Pause

There's a lot of work to be done. Stamping out heathen decadence.

Nell How much did you get today, then? Stamping.

Mrs Farley Well...

Nell Go on.

Mrs Farley I've not earnt a penny. What am I going to do? I could starve!

Nell That's 'cos you don't know how to work a crowd. I sold oysters with me sister. We had a patter. Crowds like patter.

Mrs Farley A patter?

Nell You know: "Oyster sucking's better than———"

Mrs Farley (*interrupting*) We spread God's plain and holy word.
Nell It's like you've got to have a bit of cunning.
Mrs Farley Cunning?
Nell To get what you want.
Mrs Farley I'm not sure. I think cunning is against my religion.
Nell God helps those who help themselves. I got meself a job at the *Cock and Pie*.
Mrs Farley I've heard about places like that.
Nell I serve strong waters to the gentlemen.
Mrs Farley I've heard it's the devil's own armpit.
Nell It has a decent, reg'lar sort of clientele.

A bellow is heard from the Cock and Pie

On the whole. You do get the odd difficult customer. There's one bloke won't take no for an answer. I told him I wouldn't go with him. Not for sixpence. I know where he's been.
Mrs Farley Where's that?
Nell With me sister, and she'd do anybody.
Mrs Farley Well, I better go.
Nell Where?
Mrs Farley It's four o'clock. That's when I used to wash my dad's collars.
Nell No point washing 'em now. You never liked washing 'em, did you?

Pause

Mrs Farley No.

They laugh

It's only I can't think what else to do.

Pause

Nell Do you know poetry? I'll give you sixpence if you teach me a bit poetry.
Mrs Farley Poetry?
Nell Can you say it?
Mrs Farley "The angel of the Lord came down and glory shone around."
Nell Brilliant.

Nell gives her sixpence. Mrs Farley takes it

That a deal then? You won't starve now.

Mrs Farley Not today. Why do you want know poetry?

Nell For a job.

Mrs Farley At the *Cock and Pie*?

Nell No. Across the street. The playhouse.

Mrs Farley The playhouse! That den of defilement! That pit of pestilence!

Nell I've seen the ladies. They've got lovely dresses.

Mrs Farley Have they?

Nell I've crept in the back. The candlelight shines their hair so their hair seems like flames. Glittering buckles on their shoes. Gold lace dresses.

Mrs Farley Lace! Do they fornicate?

Nell Fuck knows. They speak poetry and walk about. (*She demonstrates, speaking in a posh voice*)
          "Oysters, oysters, by the shell or by the cup.
          Slide 'em down your gullet to keep your pecker up."

Mrs Farley And they want ladies?

Nell Just one.

Mrs Farley Just one. Oh.

Nell I heard 'em talking. In the pub. Teach me now.

Mrs Farley I need to fetch things. A book of poetry. From my lodgings.

Nell I'll come with you.

Mrs Farley No. It's not far. You wait. I'll meet you back here. (*She moves to the exit*)

Nell I'll wait then. (*She calls after her*) Here, I don't know your name.

Mrs Farley Elizabeth. Elizabeth Farley.

Nell And I'm Nellie. Nellie Gwyn.

Mrs Farley exits

Nell goes over to the pub and shouts in

You can stuff your poxy job! (*She waits. She talks to herself*) They want a lady. Lady Nell. Oysters… oysters… and glory shone around. You need a patter. It's like you've got to have a bit of cunning. Cunning? (*She jumps up and looks about her*) Fuck. I've been bleedin' had.

Nell runs off

SCENE 3

Doll enters

Doll (*addressing the audience*) I wouldn't be a liar if I told you this place used to be packed to the nines. They all sat squashed on benches, which greatly facilitated the wandering of hands down breeches and bodices. Often the talk was like the roar of water and drowned out the stage. In winter you froze and in summer you cooked. It was a foul place really, but the punters came back and back time after time, louts and lords, lords and louts; who could tell the difference? Not so long back they burnt these places to the ground and pissed on the ashes. They swore they'd seen the last of them. But they sprung up again. Like mushrooms.

Nell enters

Nell (*singing*) Sixpence each.
                    Will you be enticed?
                    Round and juicy.
                    Cheap at the price.
Doll It was a moral cesspit.
Nell Oranges, Doll, I'm talking about oranges! (*She produces some oranges*) Anything I get over the sixpence I keep for myself. I get tips cos of my song. I made it up.
Doll I don't like it.
Nell You don't like nothing.
Doll I'm bitter. I've sold every tooth in my head.
Nell What's the play today?
Doll *The Fatal Maiden*. Or something.

Doll goes off

Nell (*rapturously*) *The Fatal Maiden!*

The Lights come up on Mrs Farley tied to a tree. She has been 'despoiled'. She is still dressed sumptuously in comparison to the last time we saw her. She poses, and sighs pitifully

Mrs Farley O piteous fate, O horrid crime

Which none can heal, not even time
He tied me to this willowy tree
I struggled but could not get free
I felt the heat of loins afire
He panted with his foul desire
I am despoiled, so must expire!
Ah. (*She dies*)

Mrs Betterton and Mrs Marshall enter. They are two Restoration actresses dressed as Amazons. They carry bows and arrows, which they fire simultaneously into the wings

Doll's cry is heard off stage

Amazon One We have avenged you, alas, too late.

They indicate Mrs Farley. They gather round the tree. They recite a poem, taking turns

Amazons   In these wild woods we sadly gather
With our bows and shields of leather
Here we espy the sorry sight
Of our late queen whose piteous plight
Doth leave her here tied to this tree
O Penthisilea, we weep for thee
And bare our breasts after three.

They beat their breasts three times and after the third beat bare a breast each

For Amazons we still remain
And live without the rule of men.
Fierce warriors both we be
And will go down in history.
All   And so the curtain falls at last.
On this our tragedy that's past.

They take their bows and exit. Mrs Farley is the last to go. As an actress she is transformed from the first demure sighting we had of her

Nell Liz! Liz!

Mrs Farley enters

Mrs Farley I'm Mrs Farley to you.

Nell Mrs Farley, then.

Mrs Farley What do you want?

Nell It's the same thing as before, Lizzie. Mrs Farley.

Mrs Farley Not that again. I've told you you've got to have the right way about you and you just haven't got it.

Nell What way?

Mrs Farley You've got to have a bit of breeding. Elegance. Class. Dancing. You're selling oranges. What more do you want?

Nell I hate oranges. What about me poem?

Mrs Farley You're never satisfied. That's your trouble. My advice is to forget it. You don't want to lead a life of disappointment, do you?

Nell I'm going to ask Mr Betterton. I'll get someone else to tell us a poem, and I'll say that and show me legs.

Mrs Farley Mr Betterton has all the girls he needs. He took on two last week. Extras.

Nell You never told me.

Mrs Farley He can't see everyone. Otherwise he'd spend his whole life auditioning. It's a popular profession with considerable advantages.

Nell I know.

Pause

You don't want me to be one—an actress.

Mrs Farley The theatre has to have some standards. If it didn't, where would I be? Begging or starving. Now, I've got to get on. I can't stand here all day chatting.

Pause

You'll thank me one day.

Mrs Farley exits

Nell watches her go

Nell I fucking won't.

Nell exits

SCENE 4

A tableau

Mrs Betterton appears as Shakespeare's Cleopatra. Doll appears as a slave or statue, holding a bowl. Mrs Marshall appears as Charmian, Mrs Farley as Iras

Cleopatra   Give me my robe, put on my crown, I have
Immortal longings in me. Now no more
The juice of Egypt's grape shall moist this lip.
Yare, yare, good Iras; quick: methinks I hear
Antony call. I see him rouse himself
To praise my noble act. I hear him mock
The luck of Cæsar, which the gods give men
To excuse their after wrath. Husband, I come:
Now to that name, my courage prove my title!
I am fire, and air; my other elements
I give to baser life. So, have you done?
Come then, and take the last warmth of my lips.
Farewell, kind Charmian, Iras, long farewell.

She kisses them. Iras falls and dies

Have I the aspic in my lips? Dost fall?
If thou and nature can so gently part,
The stroke of death is as a lover's pinch,
Which hurts and is desir'd. Dost thou lie still?
If thus thou vanishest, thou tell'st the world
It is not worth leave-taking.

Charmian   Dissolve, thick cloud, and rain, that I may say,
The gods themselves do weep!

Cleopatra   This proves me base:
If she first meet the curled Antony,

He'll make demand of her, and spend that kiss
Which is my heaven to have. Come thou mortal wretch,
(*To an asp which she applies to her breast*) With thy
sharp teeth this knot intrinsicate
Of life at once untie: poor venomous fool,
Be angry, and despatch. O, couldst thou speak,
That I might hear thee call great Caesar ass,
Unpolicied!

Charmian   O Eastern Star!
Cleopatra   Peace! Peace!
Dost thou not see my baby at my breast,
That sucks the nurse asleep?
Charmian   O break, O break!
Cleopatra   As sweet as balm, as soft as air, as gentle.
O Antony! Nay I will take thee too. (*She applies another asp to her arm*)
What should I stay—— (*She falls and dies*)
Charmian   In this vile world? So fare thee well.
Now boast thee, death, in thy possession lies
A lass unparallel'd. Downy windows, close,
And golden Phoebus never be beheld
Of eyes again so royal! Your crown's awry,
I'll mend it, and then play. (*She applies an asp*)
O, come apace, despatch, I partly feel thee.
It is well done, and fitting for a princess
Descended of so many royal kings. (*She dies*)

Tableau holds

And then Mrs Betterton takes her bow and exits

Mrs Marshall and Mrs Farley take their bows. Doll stands by

Mrs Marshall (*whispering*) Did you hear that?
Mrs Farley (*whispering*) Ignore it.
Mrs Marshall (*whispering*) I'm going to say something.
Mrs Farley (*whispering*) No!

Mrs Marshall harangues an unseen member of the audience

Mrs Marshall Bastard! Poxy prick!
You are no gentleman!
Is there no one here who will run him through?
I've a mind to see his guts!

Mrs Farley looks aghast

Doll Shut up.
Mrs Marshall He started it.
Doll Shut up.
Mrs Marshall Pointing at me, slandering me.
Doll I expect his lordship's a little inebriated.
Mrs Marshall He's pissed as fuck.
Doll We don't want trouble.
Mrs Farley You're making a show of yourself.
Mrs Marshall Miserable cheating impotent swine!
Doll Good evening.

Doll and Mrs Farley escort Mrs Marshall as they all exit

SCENE 5

Tiring Room

The actresses are gathered. Mrs Betterton addresses them

Mrs Betterton First, pot.
Doll I emptied it Tuesday.
Mrs Betterton And now it is Friday. Mr Betterton's wishes are that it is
to be emptied on a daily basis. He is the senior actor here and his orders
come from higher up. From Mr Killegrew and beyond him King Charles
the Second of England, Ireland, Scotland and the imperial conquests.
Doll What's he care about a piss pot?
Mrs Betterton Am I to be contradicted?
Doll No, ma'am.
Mrs Betterton Good. Then I will proceed with precipitation.

*Doll picks up the pot and empties it unceremoniously just off. She almost
bumps into Mrs Farley*

Mrs Farley Careful!

Mrs Betterton (*reading*) The forthcoming season of works to be performed by the King's Company in the summer of this year sixteen-sixty-nine shall be as follows; Item, *Sir Fopling Flutter*, a comic drama by Mr Etherege in which a modern girl desires and achieves a husband of her own choosing. An unlikely play set in town. Item, *The Reluctant Shepherdess*, a pastoral epic of small moral dimension for which we shall hire extra ribald shepherds. Item, *The Provoked Wife*, a well-observed comedy by the venerable Mr Vanbrugh. Item one, two and three, *Macbeth the Murderer*, *Othello the Moor* and *Hamlet the Ditherer* by our own Mr Shakespeare. Desdemona to be played by Mrs Marshall. Ophelia by Mrs Farley. Lady Macbeth by myself, Mrs Betterton. Mr Betterton will of course play the Thane, the Moor and in the absence of Mr Hart, The Dane.

Pause

In the event of an actress failing to attend a performance, management retains the right of instant dismissal or on production of a decent excuse, confiscation of wages. And while we at the King's would wish no great catastrophe upon our rivals at the Duke's, neither will we be praying that funds be forthcoming for the repair of their roof.

All Amen.

Mrs Betterton As to the incident following our final performance of *Antony and Cleopatra*, Mr Betterton has decreed that no more is to be said on the matter. Not a word. Is that understood?

Pause

May the Muse attend us.

Mrs Betterton exits

The actresses wait till she goes

Mrs Marshall Whore, he called me.
Doll It's his vengeance.
Mrs Farley Vengeance?
Mrs Marshall But it's me that should have the vengeance.
Doll Earl.

Mrs Marshall What?

Doll You often get that sort of behaviour off of an Earl, I've noticed. It's just their way. He'll keep on at you and on at you. Like a wolf at a carcass. He'll never let up.

Mrs Farley Why was he shouting?

Mrs Marshall He used to come in here. He paid. To watch us. Changing.

Doll Not me. I ain't taken nothing off for ten years.

Mrs Marshall Then he wanted to have me.

Doll She didn't fancy it.

Mrs Marshall He was a dog. But he persisted. So I said "Marry me and I'll do it". Thinking he'd go cock his leg up another tree.

Doll But he agreed.

Mrs Farley He agreed!

Mrs Marshall So I borrowed a costume.

Doll Desdemona, weren't it?

Mrs Marshall And I met him at a church in a small country village.

Doll Lewish-ham.

Mrs Marshall And we were married by a priest. I thought if he's fool enough to make me wife I'll take him for what I can get. So he had his night... And when I woke up the next morning he was gone.

Mrs Farley Gone?

Doll Scarpered.

Mrs Marshall The priest was no priest.

Doll He was a bleedin' actor.

Mrs Marshall I knew I'd seen his face.

Doll Earls, they go to any length. They got time on their hands, see.

Mrs Marshall I complained to the King. Lot of good it did.

Doll Lie low, I said.

Mrs Marshall And now I am publicly insulted.

Doll Hounded.

Pause

Mrs Farley If I wanted to, could I borrow a costume?

They look at her

   I was just asking.

Doll He could ruin you. Keep coming here, heckling. I seen it before.

Mrs Marshall He'll get bored.
Doll Will he?
Mrs Marshall I could meet him. Talk, settle it.
Doll You got trouble.
Mrs Marshall I'll settle it.

SCENE 6

On stage before a performance

Mrs Betterton enters, tended by Doll. Mrs Betterton moves c and begins to declaim in the grand old way. She is quite terrifying

Mrs Betterton I have given suck
        And know how tender tis to love the babe that milks me.
        I would, while it was smiling in my face
        have plucked my nipple from its boneless gums
        and dashed its brains had I so sworn as thou
        have done to this.
Doll Lord!
Mrs Betterton A fellow began to shake. He was in the front row there. (*She points*) He shook from head to foot and crossed himself.
Doll It's the way your eyes burn.
Mrs Betterton Eyes are the windows to the soul. A lot of it's in the eyes. Mr Betterton swears by them.
Doll What do you want doing today?
Mrs Betterton Widow.
Doll It's the black then. I'll get the black out. (*She may fetch an item of costume*) I don't like to say nothing but I feel I must. Our costumes ain't what they were.
Mrs Betterton We haven't got money to cast to the four winds. This is the theatre.
Doll But Mr Betterton had a new costume delivered Friday. With feathers.
Mrs Betterton Mr Betterton has given his life's blood to this company, Doll Common, let me remind you.
Doll I am reminded.
Mrs Betterton One's life's blood is one's very heart and soul. Sap, breath, everything.

Doll No offence intended, ma'am.

Mrs Betterton Mr Betterton is entitled to a few feathers, surely.

Doll He's entitled to a whole pillow.

Mrs Betterton Sometimes I wonder what would happen to a person if it was taken away. That thing one gives one's life blood for.

Doll I've never had the chance to give nothing. I'm always the dead one under the cloak, or else I'm sweeping.

Mrs Betterton I imagine it would be terrible, terrible.

Doll Still, I'm not complaining. What you've never had you can't miss. We better go in, fix you up.

Mrs Betterton Just another minute.

Pause

Have you ever noticed how quiet it is in here, before? It's as if the air's resting.

> "The raven himself is hoarse
> That croaks the fatal entrance of Duncan
> Under my battlements!"

Nell enters from the shadows

Nell I want to do that.

Doll Who's there?

Nell Will you show me? How to do it?

Doll It's orange moll. Mrs Betterton hasn't got time to waste on the likes of you. Get going!

Nell I said a poem.

Pause

I said it and Mr Betterton said I was to have a go. Saying something.

Mrs Betterton A line?

Nell Yes.

Mrs Betterton He never mentioned it to me.

Nell "A line", he said.

Mrs Betterton I suppose there's a few lines going.

Doll Nothing fancy.

Mrs Betterton I've only got fourteen myself. Have you any rural experience?

Nell Me mum kept a hen.

Mrs Betterton Well then, there's the lusty shepherdess.

Nell I'll take anything.

Mrs Betterton (*saying the line*) "Here stroll I the live long day
          Watching my fellows fork the hay."

Nell Here stroll I...

Mrs Betterton And now I must prepare myself.

Doll Some of us have preparation to do!

*Doll and Mrs Betterton go to the exit. Nell attempts her line as they are
leaving. It is very flat and mumbled. It stops Mrs Betterton in her tracks*

Nell ...the live long day.

Mrs Betterton Never underestimate the value of opening one's mouth
     while speaking. One may go a long way in the theatre with an open mouth.

Doll And not just in the theatre.

Nell opens her mouth, but gestures wildly

Nell Watching my fellows fork the hay.

Mrs Betterton A word. Stillness.

Nell Stillness?

Mrs Betterton (*with stillness*) "Here I stroll the live long day
          Watching my fellows fork the hay."
     See?

Nell Oh yeah.

Mrs Betterton A simple technique which may upon occasion be used to
     stunning advantage. As a child I was encouraged to sit still for long
     periods of time. I've found that invaluable.

Nell I never sat still. I had worms.

Mrs Betterton You may also have noticed that my head was at ten to
     eleven.

Nell Your head?

Mrs Betterton If you imagine the stage as a clock. I shall demonstrate.
     (*She demonstrates putting her head in the correct positions*) Submis-
     sion is well expressed at six o'clock. Shame at twenty to seven. Despair
     at five past twelve; not to be confused with heavenly abandonment at
     midday exactly. Death by strangulation is one of the only occasions on
     which an actress may employ a quarter to three.

Nell I see.

Mrs Betterton The best way for an artist to improve their craft is by careful observation of a seasoned and expert colleague. You may observe me.

Nell Thank you.

Mrs Betterton Follow on. You are honoured in joining a profession of much heart and great decorum.

They move to the exit. Doll does not allow Nell to follow directly after Mrs Betterton

Doll After me. And just remember, for every queen there are thirty friends at the banquet...

They exit

SCENE 7

The Tiring Room

Mrs Marshall and Mrs Farley do each other's laces

Mrs Farley I laughed and laughed and laughed. I couldn't stop laughing. He drank down a whole flask, and the rest of them beat the tables with their fists, and the noise was deafening, and then this woman came in, and you should have seen the state of her: she had a black eye, and her hair was matted, and she had bare feet, and they got her to sing in front of the King; only, she couldn't sing a note, and I laughed so much I cried; I don't know where they got her; off the streets—I think—and I never went home last night—I stayed away all night. What did you do?

Mrs Marshall Nothing. I'd sent word to the Earl of Oxford asking for a meeting. I waited in.

Mrs Farley And?

Mrs Marshall I got bored and went out. To a salon.

Mrs Farley A what?

Mrs Marshall Salon. In some very nice rooms. With interesting people; philosophers, wits, poets. You drink coffee and you talk.

Mrs Farley Talk? What about?

Mrs Marshall Ideas. Thoughts. Discoveries. They now know that the human heart has four separate compartments.

Mrs Farley Ugh!

Mrs Marshall It's science.

Mrs Farley What do they want you there for?

Mrs Marshall I'm an actress. They've never had one of those before. I'm a novelty. They ask me things.

Mrs Farley Ask you things?

Mrs Marshall About plays. About me. About life here. How we strut and fret our hour upon the stage. I like it there. It's the sort of place you can say anything. I've said things I never even knew I thought. And people listened.

Mrs Farley I never went home last night, I went somewhere else. And I'm going there again.

Mrs Betterton enters with Nell and Doll

Nell stands amid the actresses

Mrs Betterton Go ahead.

Nell I am new.

Mrs Betterton Speak up.

Nell I am new.

They look at her

Mrs Farley You!

Mrs Betterton Engaged by Mr Betterton for a try out.

Doll (*mimicking*) Here I stroll...

Mrs Marshall She's not on with me is she?

Mrs Betterton (*introducing*) Mrs Marshall, Mrs Farley. Mrs Gwyn.

Pause

The latter follows on the former. It is all easily done.

Pause

Well, well.

Mrs Marshall She'd better be proficient.

Noises are heard off stage

Mrs Betterton See to that, Doll.

Doll goes over to the door

> An audience's place is in the auditorium. Goodness only knows what
> the attraction is back here.

Mrs Marshall One can only wonder.

Doll moves back from the door

Doll Like flies round——
Mrs Farley (*interrupting*) A honey pot.

Doll goes over to the door

Doll Bugger off! You're not coming in. There's ladies changing in here.

The noise surges

> You can wait till after and it'll cost ya.

The noise surges again

> They won't listen to me. They've no respect for a body.

Mrs Marshall goes over

Mrs Marshall Shut up, you rollicking load of ball-driven fuckwits.

The noise stops; Mrs Marshall resumes her preparations

Nell I got a good one. For swearing.

They all focus on her

> We had it where I used to work.

Pause

> Turnip bollocks.

*This falls flat. They resume tasks, except for Mrs Farley. She beckons
Nell over*

Mrs Farley Come here.

Nell moves to her

Mrs Farley Show me your petticoat.
Nell What for?
Mrs Farley Show me.

Nell lifts up her skirt to reveal it. It's of greyish cloth. Mrs Farley laughs

    What a rag.
Nell What's wrong with it?

Mrs Farley pulls up her skirt to reveal her petticoat

    That's beautiful.
Mrs Farley A gift. From an admirer.
Nell It's fucking beautiful.
Mrs Farley You could wear this in a palace.
Nell Yeah.

Mrs Farley points to Nell's petticoat

Mrs Farley People don't want to pay to see that. That's like paying to see
    a dishcloth. An actress has to have the correct accoutrements. That's
    French.
Nell Blimey.
Mrs Farley Didn't he tell you about accoutrements at the audition?
Nell No.
Mrs Farley He did me. Liar.
Nell What?
Mrs Farley You never had one, did you? Did you?
Nell No.
Mrs Farley You wouldn't listen to me, would you? We work hard for
    what we got. We don't need amateurs to ruin it for us.
Nell I won't ruin it.
Mrs Farley You don't know what it's like—hundreds of faces looking

at you. You don't know what that silence is like before you speak. The
King's in today.

Nell He's not?

Mrs Farley Yes. He's come to see me. He thinks I look continental. He
gave me this. (*She signals her petticoat*) I've been to the palace. There's
special stairs round the back. They give you a candle and up you go.
Next, I'm getting shoes.

Nell Shoes… Are you going to tell on me?

Mrs Farley Too late. You're on.

Mrs Marshall approaches

Mrs Marshall (*to Nell*) You know what you have to do. Follow me on
shortly. Don't muck it up. You look like a bleedin' ghost. Come on.

Pause

Well, say something.

Nell Turnip bollocks.

Mrs Marshall God.

They exit

Scene 8

Mrs Marshall is alone on stage, performing

Mrs Marshall Here have I flown to this lonely forest
          Fled shame, dishonour and a passion torrid.
          Will I ever leave this wilderness?
          What my fate will be I fear to guess.
          My heart is beating strangely fast
          Shall I find relief at last? (*She draws out a dagger*)
          This dagger I may employ to end my sorrow
          Yet pity says wait until the morrow.
          For surely salvation swift may come
          With the sweet and rising sun. (*An idea strikes her*)
          I shall call upon the Muses three
          To aid me in my misery.

Doll, Mrs Betterton and Mrs Farley enter as Muses

Mrs Betterton Who calls us from our heavenly nest?
Mrs Marshall Tis I.
Mrs Betterton Then ask what you will of the Muses three,
        Of music.
Mrs Farley   Dancing.
Doll   And poet-ry.
Mrs Marshall My life is nothing to me now.
Mrs Betterton Do not bend beneath your woe
        Seek out friendship, hope will flow.
        Now look, here comes a shepherdess
        She will give succour to your distress.

Nell enters. She comes closer and stares at the audience, terrified

Mrs Marshall Good lady I have some small request
        May I take shelter at your bower
        And while away the cold night hour?

There is a dreadful silence. Nell gives a wail

Mrs Betterton We can no longer stay.
        Sisters, away, away, away...

Mrs Betterton, Doll, and Mrs Farley exit

Mrs Marshall May I take shelter at your bower
        And while away the cold night hour?

Nell is frozen

Mrs Marshall exits

Nell still seems frozen. After a while she begins to dance a jig. She gets livelier, warming to her task. The audience warm to her

She dances off, triumphant

SCENE 9

The Tiring Room

Mrs Betterton, Doll and Mrs Farley enter. Mrs Marshall enters very shortly after

Mrs Betterton (*scandalised*) Mrs Marshall!
Mrs Marshall I just left her out there.
Mrs Betterton Shameful!
Mrs Marshall I said my lines and waited for hers. She just stood rooted to the spot. People shouting, hissing! She kept doing funny things with her head.
Mrs Betterton She should of been at twenty to six.
Mrs Marshall What?
Mrs Betterton Mr Betterton has made a rare error in choosing her.
Mrs Farley No, he hasn't.
Mrs Marshall You can hardly call her a natural.
Mrs Betterton It seems so. She has allowed personal feelings to destroy her performance. Mr Betterton once led the entire English army with a thorn in his foot. He never manifested a twinge. Later I had to dig it out with a cheese knife.
Mrs Farley He never chose her. You did.
Mrs Betterton I?
Mrs Farley She lied. She never saw him.
Mrs Betterton Never saw him? She said she was to have a line. That is what she said. Didn't she?
Doll I took it with a pinch of salt.
Mrs Betterton I am thunderstruck. Mr Betterton!
Doll He will not be gratified.
Mrs Marshall (*to Mrs Farley*) You could have said something.
Mrs Betterton I have gone over his head by misadventure. Lord! Lord!
Doll And with royalty in.
Mrs Marshall It's us that look like fools.
Mrs Betterton Terrible! A line. She said.

Nell enters slowly, dazed

They all watch her

Mrs Marshall You showed me right up, you silly cow.
Mrs Farley Beg your old job back, if you don't want to starve.
Mrs Betterton I'm afraid you will not do.
Doll Impostor!

Nell seems in a trance

Nell I could not do it. You lot buggered off and left me.
Mrs Farley I told you, didn't I?
Nell Everything swayed as if it was wind in a forest and people were
hissing and that was like the sound of wind. And I felt like a small thing
that the wind was carrying, carrying somewhere, away, far away...
Then a thought came into my head like a shout. It said do something and
fucking hurry up about it. So I danced a little jig which I made up on the
spot out of my head and slowly all the whistling, hissing, stopped, and
then someone started to clap, and then they all clapped. Laughed and
clapped.
Mrs Marshall They laughed and clapped?
Nell I felt like I had fire inside me or whisky.
Mrs Betterton A reprieve! He may even keep you.
Nell Will he?
Mrs Farley There's no accounting for taste.
Mrs Betterton All for a jig. Well, well, it has not turned out too badly.
Mrs Marshall For her. I'm sure I've appeared to greater advantage. (*To
Doll*) Give us a rip. (*She takes her handkerchief from around her neck
and holds it out*) I get taken against my will in the second half.
Doll Anything to oblige.
Mrs Marshall Ta.

Sounds are heard from outside

Doll That's what they're like, animals. (*She nods towards Nell*) They get
a sniff of it and they go wild.
Mrs Marshall I'll see to it.

Mrs Marshall exits

Nell (*to Mrs Farley*) I did not mind the faces. I liked them. Like warm
moons shining at me. And in a special box, a man in glitter, cheering.

Mrs Farley A man in glitter?
Doll The King.
Mrs Farley He couldn't have been cheering. How's my face?
Doll It's the same one you went on with.
Mrs Farley Is it smudged?
Doll My eyes are bad. I can't do detail.

Mrs Marshall enters. She is covered in muck, especially her hair

Mrs Marshall Stink! Stink!

They all stare

In my hair. Crap from the road. Get it off me!
Mrs Farley Ugh!
Mrs Betterton This is real!
Doll (*sniffing*) Certainly.
Mrs Marshall Outside. Two men. He sent them. Bastards. Thugs. Pulled me out. "This is from the Earl of Oxford", they said. Then they rubbed shit into my hair. To teach me my manners. He sent them.
Nell It's all in her hair.
Mrs Marshall Get it off me!
Mrs Betterton (*to Doll*) It must be washed off.
Doll What did I say? At you and at you like a wolf!

Mrs Marshall gives a cry of frustration

Doll leads her away. Mrs Farley follows. They exit

Mrs Betterton (*whispering to Nell*) Did you observe?
Nell Observe?
Mrs Betterton Her head. Half past six, child, half past six. Anger. Anger and the desire for vengeance.

SCENE 10

The Tiring Room

The next day, Sunday

Mrs Betterton is rehearsing with Doll. She hands Doll her part

Mrs Betterton I am Widow Welfed. It is a small part with quite a lot of belching. (*To Doll*) Are you ready?
Doll I'm not doing any funny voices.
Mrs Betterton I don't require any.

Doll begins as Squire Squeamish

Doll Good day, Widow Welfed.
Mrs Betterton Good day, Squire Squeamish. (*She belches throughout at short intervals*) Please excuse me, it is barely past midday and I have already consumed several birds of rare plumage. The last put up quite a struggle and would not go down. Squire, Squire, you grow quite pale and seem to require salts.
Doll Salts! You would not eat me?
Mrs Betterton Oh Squire, I would never consider the consumption of my own species.
Doll Pray, madam, what species is that?
Mrs Betterton A widow, Squire. A widow with appetite! Do not tremble, nor rattle the door in a vain pretence of escape. I am no mere morsel! I am a red-blooded creature. Take your chance now while the servants are at market.
Doll There is a loud cry as if he has fallen from a great height.
Mrs Betterton He has leapt from the window. Extraordinary!
Doll I can't do cries. I'd show myself up.
Mrs Betterton That was quite satisfactory.
Doll How could she stoop to that Squire?
Mrs Betterton It is the task of an actress to discover the motivation latent in every role.
Doll But he's a row short of a full house.
Mrs Betterton I refer you to my earlier remark.
Doll I wouldn't have touched him, not if his arse was hung in diamonds.
Mrs Betterton Quite.
Doll This is our seventh. I been counting.
Mrs Betterton Seventh?
Doll Widow.
Mrs Betterton You've no business, counting. Did you have permission to count?
Doll No. Ma'am.

Mrs Betterton No.

Pause

In any case it's six. Six widows.

Doll Seven, if you count the feeble-brained spinster.

Mrs Betterton Well, I am not counting her. She is an altogether different question.

Doll When are we doing the queen again? The Scottish one.

Mrs Betterton Soon, soon. Rest assured.

Doll I like her. She's horrible.

Mrs Betterton If I asked you a question would you give me an honest answer?

Doll Cross my heart and spit on a corpse.

Mrs Betterton Am I old?

Doll No.

Mrs Betterton Good.

Doll Not compared to me.

Mrs Betterton Mr Betterton said "We are getting older". I could hardly believe he was talking to me.

Pause

(*She brings out a candle*) This is the most wonderful scene. The queen has become a child. She sings rhymes. "The Thane of Fife had a wife…" Why did she go mad, Doll?

Doll She killed a couple of geezers. It done her head in.

Mrs Betterton Could be. Could be.

Mrs Marshall enters

Doll What you doing here? It's Sunday.

Mrs Marshall (*referring to the candle*) I need that.

Doll It's a company asset.

Mrs Marshall Give it to me.

Mrs Marshall attempts to take the candle, but Doll refuses to hand it over

Doll Don't get vicious.

She hands over the candle. Mrs Marshall takes it and begins carving it with a small knife

What you doing?
Mrs Marshall Nothing.
Doll Looks like nothing.

Mrs Farley enters

Mrs Farley I didn't think there'd be anyone here.
Doll Me and Mrs Betterton have been practising. (*She refers to Mrs Marshall*) She's taking a knife to theatrical property.

Mrs Farley begins to hunt about for bits of costume in order to add to her own for glamour's sake. She holds something up to herself, a shawl

Mrs Betterton I hope you're not entertaining the notion of leaving this establishment attired in thespian habiliments.
Mrs Farley What?
Doll In your costume.
Mrs Betterton Mr Betterton has prohibited the wearing of such apparel outside of working hours due to the fact that they are returned lamentably besmirched.
Mrs Farley I've got a *rendez-vous*. An extremely important *rendez-vous*. I can't go in rags.
Doll Shall I get it off her? I have three long nails.
Mrs Betterton No, no. Such a strategy may entail further damage to company property.
Mrs Farley I'm surprised we don't go around naked on the pittance we get here.
Mrs Betterton Pecuniary considerations should hardly concern us.
Mrs Farley Why? It's not as if it's a part-time occupation. If I'm not performing, I'm learning lines. Two plays a week.
Mrs Betterton Of course. We are artists. Artists work for the love of their craft. Artists would work for nothing.
Mrs Farley Nothing!
Mrs Betterton It's a calling.
Mrs Farley You can't live on a calling. Air's the only thing that's free and you can starve on that.

Mrs Betterton People come here, high born and low. They come to our
theatre to partake in the sublime. To be part of that peculiar something
that uplifts and transforms. To see real actors perform.
Mrs Farley Real actors? I'm real, aren't I?
Mrs Betterton You!

Pause

You are free to spend your free time as you choose. But not in our
costumes. So, kindly remove them now.
Mrs Farley You can't tell me what to do.
Mrs Betterton This is tedious.
Mrs Farley They don't come to see you. They come to see us.
Mrs Betterton Us?
Doll Don't take no notice of her.
Mrs Betterton Us?
Mrs Farley The young ones. With decent legs.
Mrs Betterton Legs.
Mrs Farley They can't get enough of it. Of us. They don't even see you.
Not really see. Everyone knows.
Mrs Betterton They see me.

Pause

Of course they do.
Doll Don't listen to her. What does she know? Mrs Betterton has come
here every day of her life. Even when it was closed down. She does
exercises with her tongue, to make the words better. I seen her. I seen
her up all night with lines. I seen her wash her hands a hundred times so
she could say it on stage and you'd believe her.
Mrs Betterton It's all right, Doll. I am aware. I am aware there are those
types. The types that come for flesh. But I am dumbstruck for you. Sorry
for you.
Mrs Farley Sorry for me?
Mrs Betterton If you have not had the joy.
Mrs Farley I'm going now. There's a carriage waiting for me. I've got
a *rendez-vous*. You've probably never had one of those.

She goes to the exit

Nell enters, running

Nell Liz!
Mrs Farley Not now. I'm late.
Nell But Liz.
Mrs Farley I can't stop now.
Nell I was told to give you this.

She hands Mrs Farley a single coin

A man gave it me, to put it into your hands.
Mrs Farley A man.
Nell A messenger. He said to tell you "parting gift".
Mrs Farley Parting gift—and that's all he gave you. This coin?
Nell That's all.

Mrs Farley sits down

Mrs Farley Parting gift. Are you sure that's what he said?
Nell Yes.

Pause

Mrs Farley And that's all he gave you?
Nell Yes.

Pause. Mrs Farley is devastated

Never mind.
Mrs Farley What do you know!

Mrs Marshall stops her carving

Mrs Marshall There. (*She holds it up*)
Nell What is it?

Mrs Marshall gives it to her

Mrs Marshall Have a look.
Nell Ain't it good! A little man. A wax man.

She tries to show Mrs Farley

Mrs Marshall Homunculus.

Nell He's got a little mouth. His mouth is open. Like a cry.

She offers it to Doll

Doll I'm not touching it. It has hair. Melted on the top.
Mrs Marshall I had a lock of his hair. The Earl of Oxford. He gave it to
   me. A love token.

Mrs Betterton also looks

Mrs Betterton Rebecca Marshall, that is evil. What are you doing now?
Mrs Marshall I'm sticking a pin in the bastard's neck.

They wince

   That is for the shit rubbed into my hair.
Nell It has gone right through!
Mrs Farley Will he feel it?

Mrs Marshall sticks another pin in

Mrs Marshall That is for crying whore!
Mrs Betterton He will be in pain.
Doll He will be in bleedin' agony.

Another pin goes in

Nell That's his bollocks.
Mrs Betterton It is witchery!

Mrs Marshall holds up the doll, c

Mrs Marshall Round about the cauldron go.
                 In the poison entrails throw.
                 Toad that under cold stone
                 Days and nights has thirty-one
                 Sweltered, sleeping, venom got
                 Boil thou first in the charm'd pot.
Mrs Betterton Fillet of a fenny snake
                 In the cauldron boil and bake.

Mrs Marshall Eye of newt and toe of frog
        Wool of bat and tongue of dog.
Mrs Betterton Adder's fork and blind worm's sting.
Mrs Farley Lizard's leg and howlet's wing.
Mrs Betterton For a charm of powerful trouble
        Like a hell broth boil and bubble.

Mrs Farley
Mrs Betterton } (*together*) Double double toil and trouble
Mrs Marshall   Fire burn and cauldron bubble.
Doll

Nell joins in with a demonic version of her jig

      Double double toil and trouble
      Fire burn and cauldron bubble.

The chant grows to a crescendo as Mrs Marshall throws the doll to the floor and tramples it underfoot

      Double double toil and trouble
      Fire burn and cauldron bubble.

Mrs Marshall Never prosper! (*She spits on it. She addresses the actresses*) He was my keeper. Now look at him.
Mrs Farley You need a keeper.
Doll You won't get another one.
Mrs Marshall I don't want another one. I had a husband once. You wouldn't have known me. I used to creep about. He liked me to be quiet. (*She picks up pieces of the doll and puts them in her pocket*)
Mrs Farley I want a drink. If he don't want me. Someone else will. Won't they?
Doll Course.
Mrs Marshall I went out last night. To a salon. Someone remarked that he'd never known of so much interest in the theatre, not since we actresses had arrived. Could I corroborate that, he asked? Oh yes, I said. Certainly. I'll corroborate it. "You'll be wanting to own the theatres next", he said. "Profits and all".

Pause

I'll have a drink too. (*To Nell*) You coming?

Nell In a bit.
Mrs Betterton I shall not be joining you. We have old friends for supper.

Mrs Betterton, Mrs Marshall and Mrs Farley exit

Doll I fancy a bit of sweeping.(*She begins to sweep*)
Nell I had a message, too. From the man. He said there is a carriage outside and I may use it at my own convenience. The special stairs...

Pause

What do you think, Doll? The King.
Doll Life's like a storm, that's what I think. Don't get in its way. That's what I think. It don't matter what anyone does, we all end up dead meat, don't we?
Nell You look on the bleedin' dark side, Doll. That's your trouble. Anyway, I decided. I'll go. Just this once, mind. I'm an actress, not a tart.

Nell exits

Doll sweeps

CURTAIN

ACT II

A performance is in progress

Nell and Mrs Marshall are in breeches, sparklingly confident, each with a sword

Nell How now, sir. You're in my path!
Mrs Marshall Nay, you are in mine, sire!
Nell I take exception to that.
Mrs Marshall And I too. Will you not step from my course?
Nell I'm buggered if I will.
Mrs Marshall Then I take you for an intolerable, plaguey rogue.
Nell And I take you for a right ambling Harry.
Mrs Marshall Will you draw, sir?
Nell Certainly.

They draw their swords

Prepare to gasp your last.
Mrs Marshall Say farewell to the sun. (*Aside*) Mind, he has a fine pair of legs for one so foul- lipped.
Nell (*aside*) I swear the oaf has a mouth the colour of cherries.

They begin to fight with gusto

Are you willing to submit to a superior striker, sirrah?
Mrs Marshall Sure it is you, sir Feeble, who must crumble!
Nell ⎫ (*together; aside*) Odd! I could swear there is some-
Mrs Marshall ⎭ thing almost womanly in the deftness, grace and expert sword wielding of this stranger.

They fight some more. They come close together, their hats fall off

Mrs Marshall I declare!
Nell Sister!
Mrs Marshall Friend!
Nell Both disguised.
Mrs Marshall Accounting for such noble limbs and lustrous eyes.
Nell   ⎫ (*together*)   Let us waste no time in further strife
Mrs Marshall ⎭   And without delay make amends
                                   It is far more profitable to be friends
                                   For us women in a land of men
                                   So let us share our victory
                                   Enjoying our mutual company

They turn to the audience

And while we're at it, playing for your pleasure
We'll ask shares in your payments for good measure
The price of our glorious forms you see
Is shares in this very company.

They laugh, bow, and exit

SCENE 2

Mrs Betterton comes forward, and addresses Mr Betterton who is unseen in the auditorium

Mrs Betterton Thomas? Thomas? It is the matter we discussed at breakfast. You remember.

Pause

I am afraid it has come up again. I know there is no precedent for it, dear. But in answer to that I have been told to reply that indeed there was no precedent for a wig till the first man did wear one. And now. Lo! There is scarcely a fellow who does not sport one. Bristly or fluffy. You cannot step out of doors nowadays but you see a periwig advancing towards you at great speed and in danger of toppling.

Pause

Sorry, I do digress.

Pause

No, my dear, we were not referring to your particular wig. How could you think so?

Pause

Dear heart, they will have shares. Shares, shares, they talk nothing but shares. They say you have shares and they will have them too. Company shares and profits.

Pause

You may say that they have got above themselves. What with all the fuss there is about them. Royalty and whatnot. Carriages and flowers, messages and hangers on. That may be the case. Indeed it may. But that does not alter the fact that they will not be dissuaded from their course. They say that the town does not come to see fusty old men in squashed hats declaim Caesar but to see actresses in the flesh, living and breathing, the real creatures.

Pause

Squashed.

Pause

Yes, I explained that it was your lucky hat, my dear, passed down through the generations.

Pause

I can't remember their reply to that.

Pause

No! It is not that I am asking. I ask only because I am asked to ask. But still, it would seem unfair to me that the others should have shares and

I none. Am I to sit in the tiring room and watch them count out their coin while I knit mittens? Why, I should not like that. Indeed no. Also, dear, we need a new cupboard for the cheeses especially, and if I have not asked you once for the means I have asked you a thousand times till I am quite worn thin with asking. And if I did have shares I should certainly know how to put the cash to good purpose. Besides, I should also like to venture a few small opinions of my own concerning artistic matters.

Pause

Indeed, Thomas, you are the one that's partial to cheese.

Doll enters

Doll What's he say?
Mrs Betterton He says he will give it his consideration. He has to answer to higher than himself, remember.

Pause

Look. (*She brings out from her pocket a long piece of yarn*)
Doll What's that?
Mrs Betterton There are three colours in it. Three yarns. You twist them together. It takes hours. Hours.
Doll It's horrible. What's it for?
Mrs Betterton I don't know. It's just a long thing. However, it keeps weary hands occupied during long plays when one's appearance is minor.

Pause

Doll? Do you ever hear things? Voices?
Doll What sort of voices?
Mrs Betterton Ethereal voices. They have told me "The waiting will not be for much longer".
Doll What waiting?
Mrs Betterton For a part. A great part. That must be their meaning.
Doll How do you know they're telling the truth? Voices can be tricksy.

Mrs Betterton Why should they lie? Besides, I have proof. See this. (*She holds out her hand*)

Doll Wedding ring.

Mrs Betterton One morning I woke up, and for the first time in thirty years it was not on my finger. They told me where to find it, and they were right.

Doll Where was it?

Mrs Betterton In the slops bucket.

Doll How'd it get in there?

Mrs Betterton I've no idea. No idea. Not to wait much longer, they said. Not much longer.

Mrs Betterton exits

Mrs Farley enters, hurrying. She has a blanket round her

Mrs Farley (to Doll) My laces, Doll. You've got to do my laces. I'm late.

Doll Patience is a virtue.

Mrs Farley (*turning her back to Doll*) Pull 'em tight, Doll.

Doll I am pulling them.

Mrs Farley That ain't tight enough.

Doll Me poor old fingers are giving out.

Mrs Farley You do it, and I'll give you threepence.

Doll Fourpence.

Mrs Farley Done.

Doll Mind. I'm not saying I can work miracles.

Doll and Mrs Farley exit

Mrs Betterton, Mrs Marshall and Nell enter. They are all made up in high Restoration style, posed in tableau

The following is an extract from The Provoked Wife. *With Mrs Marshall as Lady Fanciful, Nell as Mademoiselle, Mrs Betterton as Cornet and Mrs Farley as Pipe. Pipe waits in the wings*

Lady Fanciful Cornet! Cornet!

Cornet enters

Cornet Ma'am?

Lady Fanciful How do I look this morning?

Cornet Your ladyship looks very ill, truly.

Lady Fanciful Lard, how ill-natured thou art, Cornet, to tell me so,
though the thing should be true. Don't you know that I have humility
enough to be but too easily out of conceit with myself? Hold the glass;
I dare swear that will have more manners than you have.—Mademoiselle, let me have your opinion too.

Mademoiselle My opinion pe, matam, dat your ladyship never look so
well in your life.

Lady Fanciful Well, the French are the prettiest obliging people; they say
the most acceptable, well-mannered things—and never flatter.

Mademoiselle Your ladyship say great justice inteed.

Lady Fanciful Nay, everything's just in my house but Cornet. The very
looking-glass gives her the *démenti*. (*She looks into her hand mirror*)
But I'm almost afraid it flatters me, it makes me look so very engaging.

Mademoiselle Matam, if de glass was burning glass, I believe your eyes
set de fire in de house.

Lady Fanciful Get out of the room, Cornet! I can't endure you, you look
so insufferably ugly.

Cornet Ma'am.

She curtsies, and exits

Lady Fanciful Have you ever been in love, Mademoiselle?

Mademoiselle (*sighing*) *Oui*, matam.

Lady Fanciful And were you beloved again?

Mademoiselle (*sighing*) No, matam.

Lady Fanciful O ye gods! What an unfortunate creature should I be in
such a case! But nature has made me nice for my own defence: I'm nice,
strangely nice, Mademoiselle; I believe were the merit of whole
mankind bestowed upon one single person, I should still think the fellow
wanted something to make it worth my while to take notice of him.

Mademoiselle Ah, matam, I wish I was fine gentleman for your sake. I
do all de ting in de world to get a leetel way into your heart. I make song,
I make verse, I give you de serenade, I give you great many present; I
no eat, I no sleep, I be lean, I be mad, I hang myself, I drown myself. *Ah,
ma chère dame, que je vous aimerais!*

Lady Fanciful Well, the French have strange obliging ways with 'em.
You may take those two pairs of gloves, Mademoiselle.

Mademoiselle Me humbly tanke my sweet lady.

Cornet enters

Cornet Here is Pipe, ma'am. To sing you a song.

Pause. Pipe does not enter

Here is Pipe, ma'am. To sing you a song.

Pause

Nell Pipe! We ain't got all day.

Pipe enters, coming forward slowly. She is now visibly pregnant. She begins to sing

Mrs Farley Fly, fly, you happy shepherds, fly... (*She stops, drying up. She tries again*) Fly, fly.
Mrs Marshall You're nothing like a pipe.
Mrs Farley I can sing, can't I?
Doll You're showing.
Mrs Farley It's not that bad.
Mrs Betterton Someone else will have to be Pipe.
Mrs Farley Who?
Mrs Betterton I expect Mr Betterton will see to it. Some new girl.
Mrs Farley I am Pipe.
Mrs Betterton You will not do. Not in your present way.
Mrs Farley I'll tie my lace tighter.
Doll You and whose army?
Mrs Farley I'm not on long. Let's get on with it. (*She sings*) Fly, fly... Come on!

The others return to the Tiring Room. Mrs Farley follows them

Mrs Betterton It is impossible. Mr Betterton will not have it. He cannot. We could lose our licence. To be that way on a public stage. There are laws.
Mrs Farley Laws!
Mrs Marshall You knew about them. If we were all as careless as you, the theatre would have to close down.

Mrs Farley It's not my fault.

Mrs Marshall Whose fault is it, then?

Mrs Farley I went back looking for the special stairs but I couldn't find them. They took me there before and it was easy, but when I went back I couldn't find them. It was like a maze. I wandered and wandered. You get tired. Where will I go?

Mrs Marshall You should have thought about that.

Mrs Farley Please.

Mrs Betterton There's no choice in the matter.

Doll You've been lucky hanging on this long.

Mrs Farley turns to Mrs Marshall

Mrs Farley Help me.

Mrs Marshall What do you mean?

Mrs Farley You know.

Doll You don't want to do that.

Mrs Farley Who asked you? (*To Mrs Marshall*) I want you to do it.

Mrs Marshall No.

Mrs Farley You've got to. Please.

Doll I knew a woman who rotted inside, after.

Nell Shut up, Doll.

Mrs Farley It's not too late, is it?

Mrs Marshall It's never too late. Have you seen it done before?

Mrs Farley No.

Mrs Betterton I've seen it done.

Mrs Marshall Sit down.

Mrs Farley sits down

Get a cloth.

Doll gets a cloth

Mrs Farley Is that for blood?

Mrs Marshall No. You put it in your mouth and bite on it.

Doll You need something sharp. Long and sharp.

Mrs Betterton fetches a long pin from a costume brooch

Mrs Betterton Here. A queen's brooch.

Mrs Marshall takes it

Mrs Marshall Give us your arm.

She takes Mrs Farley's arm. She sticks the pin into it. Mrs Farley cries out

Mrs Farley Ah!
Mrs Marshall That's nothing. Still want it done?

Pause. Mrs Farley nods. The women close round her

Mrs Farley Hold my hand, someone.

Nell holds her hand. They begin. Mrs Farley gives a more awful cry. Then a worse cry

   No! (*She takes the rag from her mouth*) I can't. I can't.

The women move away from her

Mrs Marshall It doesn't always work.

Pause

Mrs Farley Before I go. Would any of you ladies care to purchase a petticoat? Well fashioned and stitched. It's pure silk. French. (*She lifts her skirt to show it*) An absolutely invaluable accoutrement. (*She takes it off and holds it out*) Well.
Mrs Betterton It's very pretty, but not to my particular taste.
Doll I'd only use it as a snot rag.
Mrs Farley It's hardly worn. What's the matter?

She waves the petticoat closer to the women; they back away so as not to be touched by it

   Superstitious? I said "It's hardly worn"!
Nell I'll buy it.

Nell gives her the money

Mrs Farley Thanks. (*She offers Nell the petticoat*)
Nell You keep it.

Mrs Farley keeps hold of it

Mrs Marshall How long are you going to live off a petticoat?
Mrs Farley Maybe you should have a care. Maybe your luck will run out.

   Mrs Farley exits

Mrs Marshall A petticoat never saved anyone.

Scene 3

The Tiring Room

Nell enters, singing to herself

Nell   Cease of cupid to complain
                  Love's a joy ev'n while a pain.
                  Charming raptures, matchless sweets
                  Love alone all joy complete.
                  Moving glances, balmy kisses
                  Oh then think how great his bliss is.

   Doll enters, dragging a sack of props

Doll Don't mind me.

Nell continues to sing

   What a bleedin' racket.

Nell hums

   What you dressed up for? We're only sorting.

Nell continues to hum, louder

Mrs Marshall enters

Nell and Mrs Marshall sing a few lines together

Mrs Betterton enters. She watches them

Doll drags things out of the sack

Three dutch collars. Patching.
Mrs Marshall Here. (*She takes them and begins to mend them*)
Mrs Betterton Three dutch collars.
Doll One spoon. Bent. In need of straightening.
Mrs Betterton See to it, Doll.

Doll bites it straight

One spoon.
Doll One crown. King's. Requiring spit and polish.
Nell I'll do that. (*She takes the crown*)
Mrs Betterton One crown...

Doll pulls something else out of the sack

Doll One soiled jerkin.
Mrs Marshall That's not ours.
Doll Ain't it?
Mrs Marshall No. It's one of theirs. From the men's tiring room. They
   slipped it into our sack.
Nell Bleedin' cheek.
Mrs Marshall It's an old trick.
Doll I'll soil it some more and slip it back.
Mrs Marshall I would.
Doll One eaglet. In need of beak and feathers.
Mrs Marshall We can't work miracles.

Doll pulls something out of the sack

Doll One maggot ridden corpse's finger.

Nell Oh God!

Doll My mistake. It's an old bread roll. I been looking for that.

Nell tosses the crown to Doll

Nell Finished.

The crown falls

Mrs Betterton Have a care!

Doll holds the crown

In the theatre we are not superstitious for nothing.

Doll I saw the old king. I saw him put his head on the block. Then whoosh.

Nell What was it like?

Doll Well, it sort of rolled off.

Nell Not that. The occasion.

Doll Crowded. (*She pulls things from the sack*) A scrap of fur. Two beads. That's the lot. The rest is curtains.

Mrs Betterton From today I shall not be attending the theatre on a regular basis.

Doll Gawd.

Mrs Betterton Mr Betterton has talked to me.

Doll You never said.

Mrs Betterton I was awaiting my moment. Timing, timing. Some younger actresses must be given a chance. People like to see them.

Doll Gawd.

Mrs Betterton They will partner Mr Betterton. We were partners for many years. Many years. (*She sits very still and does not move*)

Nell She's not moving.

Mrs Marshall Leave her.

Doll Mrs B? Mrs B? I'll have to tell Mr Betterton.

Mrs Marshall No. Then he'd never let her come again.

Nell Mrs Betterton? Mrs Betterton?

Mrs Marshall She'll come to herself.

Mrs Betterton I used to work in the wardrobe. And I used to watch and watch and wonder what it would be like. You know, to...

Nell What?

Doll Do it. The acting.

Mrs Betterton I used to help my husband with his lines. And naturally, I learnt them too. Then one day, he was playing Othello, and his Iago fell sick. He ate something that disagreed with him. A pork pie. Anyway, it was rotten. Mr Betterton was caught short and could not find anyone else at such little notice to do the part. Except for me. I'd read it with him many times. We knew it could mean trouble if the bishops found me out, being a woman, but we were younger and reckless and we thought no-one would ever know.

Nell What happened?

Mrs Betterton We got away with it. We were very close, Mr Betterton and I, and it was as if I hung off his breath, and he off mine, and the words flew between us. That was my first time.

Pause

After that we did it on a regular basis. My fool to his Lear, his Falstaff to my Hal. And then, of course, the day came when everything changed and for the first time we women were permitted by Royal decree to act upon a stage. A great stir it caused. And I was one of the first ever and when I spoke, a great hush descended on the house, and it was as if the men and women gathered there were watching a miracle, like water turning to wine or a sick man coming to health.

Pause

It was then I knew that I had done a terrible thing and that nothing would ever be the same for me again. I had tasted a forbidden fruit and its poisons had sunk deep into my soul. You see, Iago is like a whip that drives the life around him, when Hal makes a choice the whole world holds its breath. I never forgot that feeling. The poison's still in my blood. Like a longing. A longing. I looked for that poison everywhere and couldn't find it. Not in the Desdemonas or Ophelias. Only in her, the dark woman.

Pause

We were partners for many years. And when he told me it was over, I swear he had tears in his eyes. I had never seen him cry before, except, of course, when the part required it.

Pause

Nell You better go home, Mrs B.

Mrs Betterton I'm waiting.

Doll Better wait at home. Not here. You don't want him finding you. He'll think you've gone funny.

Mrs Betterton I've never missed a cue.

Nell We know that. We know.

Mrs Marshall You can't stay sitting here.

Mrs Betterton Then I shall approach my husband once more for tomorrow's performance. I am not above a woman selling artichokes.

Mrs Betterton exits

Mrs Marshall The first time I was ever in a theatre I saw her. Somehow she just knew how to do things. Even the business with the bloody clocks.

Doll Fate is a wicked thing. Time don't have pity on no-one. No-one.

SCENE 4

Outside the theatre, some time later

Mrs Farley is standing alone. She looks ill, dirty, bedraggled, weak. She is clad in her petticoat, which is dirty, ragged

Mrs Farley Two pence. Two pence. I do anything. You can punch me. Look! (*She shows her arms, which are bruised*) Nothing. Stood here all afternoon. Nothing doing. Should have washed my face. Tired. Too tired to do it. I might have done better business if I had.

Pause

It's not me. It's them. They're not doing their job properly. The blokes aren't coming out excited. They're coming out limp. They're not coming out looking for it. I should be in there. Not outside.

Pause

Thing is, I'm better now. Better than I was. That's the pity of it. I've learnt things out here. The art of performance. You can't act tired, not for business purposes. You've got to act like you like it. Love it even. You learn that. Out here I'm a real pro.

Pause

I left it. Had to. Little white body. Laid it on some steps. What a cry when I left it.

Pause

I'm going to find a gutter or a corner and lie down. Not in the street! Yes. Right here in the street. (*She begins to wander off*) It's getting dark, dark.

She exits

SCENE 5

The Tiring Room

Doll and Nell are present

Doll I looks out the window. I sees her. Feeding off the leavings.
Nell Don't be morbid. Do my hair.
Doll Do it yourself.
Nell You watch it.
Doll It ain't for a part, is it?
Nell I'm going out.
Doll Well, I ain't employed to tart you up for private shenanigans.
Nell I'll do it myself, then. (*She begins to do her hair*)
Doll Them new shoes?
Nell What you hanging round for?
Doll Do things. For her. Errands. Things to collect up. Breaks my heart.
Nell Here. (*She gives her a cup*)
Doll What is it?
Nell Sherry.
Doll You won't get rid of me by poison.

Nell Don't be daft. It ain't poison. (*She drinks some*) See?

Doll A cup of sherry... (*She sips some*) I thought you was only going once.

Nell You're not paid to think, are you?

Doll Here's her parts. (*She shows her a bag of scrolls*) I have to give 'em in. To her.

Nell Who?

Mrs Marshall enters

Doll (*loudly*) Her! (*She shoves the bag at Mrs Marshall*) Here y'are. Assorted queens and wives. Faithful have a blue star, unfaithful a red circle.

Mrs Marshall Parts?

Doll She's had 'em years. (*She drinks some more*)

Mrs Marshall Nell, we are no longer hirelings.

Doll Starlings?

Mrs Marshall Hirelings. Hirelings. (*To Nell*) Me and you, Nell. We are shareholders.

Nell Fuck!

Mrs Marshall It has been agreed. We have shares.

Doll I thought you said "Starlings".

Nell Cheers.

She takes a cup and drinks. She hands it to Mrs Marshall

Shareholders!

Mrs Marshall Shareholders!

They celebrate

Doll I helped her with them parts. I helped her for so long I forgot I couldn't read.

Nell They saw sense then. I'll drink to that tonight. (*She picks up a shawl, in preparation for leaving*)

Mrs Marshall You don't have to go now.

Nell Don't have to?

Mrs Marshall Your *rendez-vous*.

Nell It's arranged.

Mrs Marshall Things have changed, Nell. As fast as that. The point is, you can choose. That's the point. You don't have to go.

Nell I want to bloody go.

Pause

It's all his hair. That hair's real. Lovely black hair.

Doll Scene shifter. He wants me as a scene shifter. I told him. I'm too old for that. I can't be doing with it. Can you see me humping a wardrobe?

Mrs Marshall Are you in love?

Nell Love? Going there. It's exciting. I'm sixteen. I want to try things. New things. I'm lucky. I've always been lucky. People say I'm beautiful, but so are lots of girls. So why me? Why me and the King? Luck. That's all. I get what I want. I always have. I had my own oyster stall at eleven. I have this thing I do. I imagine. I imagine what I want and then I get it. Somehow I get it. It just seems to go on and on and on. And I became an actress and I got the King.

Mrs Marshall I imagine things, too. I imagined not having a keeper. Freedom.

Nell And you got it. We're different, that's all. I'm free to do what I want, and you are too.

Mrs Marshall Free. To play a faithful wife or an unfaithful wife. A whore, a mistress. We play at being what we are. Where's the freedom in that?

Nell How d'you mean?

Mrs Marshall But now I'm none of those things, so what am I?

Doll Tastes of fucking horse piss.

Nell Don't drink it if you don't like it!

Mrs Marshall (*to Nell*) Now we've got the chance to be something different, new. Do you see?

Doll She ain't got no chances to be nothing.

Nell Stay out of it, Doll.

Doll No chances left. That's the point.

Nell (*to Mrs Marshall*) Don't take no notice of her.

Doll I got me faculties. I'm telling her.

Mrs Marshall Telling me?

Nell She's pissed.

Doll Someone has spoken out of turn. Said something. Betrayed you.

Mrs Marshall Betrayed me?

Doll He knows about the little wax man. The witchery.

Nell Who does?

Doll The Earl of Oxford.

Mrs Marshall Who said something?
Doll I never opened me mouth.
Nell What can he do? The Earl.
Doll They're still up to burning people.
Nell Burning them?
Doll Not a pleasant way to go.
Nell They wouldn't do that.
Mrs Marshall Wouldn't they? He hates me.

Pause

I have to go. I can see that.
Nell We got shares now.
Doll Shares!
Mrs Marshall I'll have to live in some bloody cold place. Hidden. Quiet.
   Keeping my mouth shut.
Nell It won't come to that.
Mrs Marshall What will it come to? Just a flogging? That gets an
   audience. Would you stay for that?

Pause

Nell Maybe you could start again, someplace.
Mrs Marshall Maybe. They found another word for me.
Doll Witch.
Mrs Marshall Before I could find one for myself. If they don't get you
   one way they get you another. (*She picks up the bag with Mrs Better-
   ton's parts*) Don't say I've been here.
Doll Leave your parts, then.
Mrs Marshall No. They're not having anything off me.

Pause

He had a bad back and three teeth pulled. Also a lump on his neck. Fuck
knows the state of his bollocks. Think of me.
Nell Good luck.
Mrs Marshall I'll burn these.
Doll Burn 'em?

Mrs Marshall indicates the parts and exits

Nell I better get a move on. I'm fucking late.

Doll Burn 'em. She said. Can't be right. Mrs Betterton's parts.

Nell Stop fucking going on. You're pissed. Look out the window. See if there's a carriage.

Doll (*singing*) I wish, I wish, but it's all in vain.
I wish I were a maid again... (*She looks out of the window*)

Nell looks in the mirror

Can't see a carriage.

Nell How do I look, Doll?

Doll I can see orange.

Nell Orange? (*She goes to look*) Fucking hell. That's fire, Doll, fire!

Doll Fire! That's it. The end. The end.

Nell Fuck.

Doll Help.

Nell gathers a few belongings

What'll we do?

Nell Shut up, I'm thinking.

Doll What'll we do now?

Nell We got to get out.

Doll Leave here?

Nell Get moving!

Doll But where'll we go?

Nell I dunno about you, but I'm joining The Duke's.

Nell runs out

Doll Oh, help! Help! It's the end. The end!

The stage darkens. Briefly, there is an orange glow, then blackness

SCENE 6

Nell is on stage at the Duke's Playhouse, glowing

Nell   This is the epilogue and let me tell ye

That none delivers it as good as Nellie.
Tis my task to give the play summation
It is indeed a test of concentration
While some declare for that I am not fit
Yet none can damn me for a lack of wit
If once I did serve gentlemen their waters
Well now I am the envy of their daughters
Yet some good citizens with apoplectic stutter
Cry "Be gad, sirs, the doxy's from the gutter"
Well I say this, it's not stopped our duller poets
(we know the agony they cause, we've all sat through it)
From using Nell's finesse and matchless charms
To add a little quality to their interminable yarns.
So 'stead of the scurrilous sentiments to which you treat me
Should be with heartfelt gratitude you greet me
For, admit it, are you not the happier and hale
To have this Nellie finish off our tale?

She curtsies and exits as if to great acclaim

SCENE 7

Nell is in her private tiring room at the Duke's

Mrs Betterton and Doll enter

Doll It's me an' her.
Mrs Betterton Us.
Doll We sneaked in round the back.
Nell Well?
Doll "Well", what?
Nell Ain't you noticed?
Doll Noticed?
Nell I'm on me own.
Doll Oh yeah.
Nell I have my own room. To myself.
Doll Innit lonely?
Nell No. It's private.
Doll What do you want to be private for?

Nell Sometimes I receive guests.

Doll Guests! More like earls from the looks of 'em. Got shares here?

Nell Not here. Still, I've come a long way, ain't I? (*She picks up some parts*) Look.

Doll What is it?

Nell It's a play.

Doll I'm sick of plays.

Nell It has a part for me. Especially written for me.

Doll What's someone want to write a part for you for?

Nell Because I am a shining light upon our stage.

Doll And I'm the Queen of Sheba's uncle.

Nell That is what she said when she put the part into my hands.

Doll Who?

Nell Mrs Behn. She is the author.

Mrs Betterton A part written for Nell!

Doll (*to Nell*) You started her off now! (*To Mrs Betterton*) A lady did it.

Mrs Betterton Can they write plays?

Doll -She has.

Mrs Betterton Is it performable?

Nell Don't be old-fashioned.

Doll Mrs B is old-fashioned.

Mrs Betterton That is correct. You may blame longevity. You know, you have done quite well for yourself.

Nell Yes, I have.

Mrs Betterton Quite well indeed. I should like to think that I had a hand in it. A little hand in it.

Nell You did. You did.

Mrs Betterton Now you are opening your mouth with competence.

Nell gives a short laugh

Nell I make half my lines up. They're quite funny.

Mrs Betterton Not so loud, dear. If Mr Betterton hears you, he may begin to notice.

Doll It's like old times. You and Mr B on stage together at the Duke's. Like you was before at the old place.

Mrs Betterton The old place...

Doll Never you mind about it, Mrs B.

Mrs Betterton (*to Nell*) You know, you have done quite well for yourself.

I should like to think I had a hand in it. I would. I would. That is like a chink of light.

Doll That's nice. A chink of light.

Mrs Betterton Let us commence.

Doll We are commencing.

Mrs Betterton Midnight.

Nell Joy.

Mrs Betterton Twenty past four.

Nell Anger.

Mrs Betterton Good, good. Deep breaths.

Nell takes a deep breath

Today's lesson. Affectation.

Doll (*to Nell*) Come on, come on, Where's our shilling. We ain't doing it for nothing.

Nell All right. All right. It's in me purse. On the side.

Doll Mrs Betterton is vastly experienced and don't do lessons for sod all.

Mrs Betterton Affectation can be described as the annoying adherence to useless and superfluous gesture and or intonation such as can be found in the lesser breed of player or duds as Mr Betterton and I were privately wont to call them.

Nell I always pay, don't I?

Doll You was gutter born and bred, and them sort don't change.

Mrs Betterton A decent performance may be utterly ruined by the players insistence on adopting a false and irritating character trait.

Nell You're getting above yourself.

Doll You is above yourself.

Mrs Betterton This often manifests itself in the laugh. (*She laughs in an irritating manner*)

Doll You are privileged to be in the presence of Mrs B's presence.

Nell Am I?

Mrs Betterton laughs again

Mrs Betterton Very trying.

Nell I don't want any more lessons.

Mrs Betterton Other culprits are the nervous cough. The over-demonstrative fan and the excessively fluttered kerchief.

Nell I don't want any more lessons.

Doll Yes, you do.
Nell No. I don't.
Doll Yes, you do.
Mrs Betterton No. She does not.

Pause

Nell He says he will buy me a house. A whole house. If I leave.
Mrs Betterton If you leave?
Nell It will have a large park attached.

Pause

Plus a couple of peacocks, a footman, cutlery, plate, silver salvers, a necklace, half a hundred weight of linen, best linen, and the loan of a horse and carriage.
Mrs Betterton That is a lot.
Doll That is a fucking fortune.
Mrs Betterton Yes, I can see that is a fucking fortune. It would be hard to turn down, I can see that.
Nell I'm not going because of what you think.
Doll Ain't you?
Nell No. I had a feeling.
Doll What you on about?
Nell I never had it before. In my gut. Like there was something there. Something curled up. Something ready to spread round my whole body.
Doll (*to Mrs Betterton*) What's she on about?
Nell I never had it before. Not like that. A feeling.
Mrs Betterton Fear.
Nell Yes. That's what it was. Fear. I woke up and then suddenly I couldn't imagine what comes next.
Doll What's happening?
Nell I tried to imagine but I couldn't.

Pause

Nothing. If I stay here I'll just grow old and then what?

Pause

A house with a park. Children.

Nell exits

Doll Bloody hell.

Mrs Betterton gets up slowly

You're not hearing them voices again?

Mrs Betterton begins to recite Lady Macbeth's final speech. She does it wonderfully in the grand old manner

Mrs Betterton Yet here's a spot. Out, damned spot! out, I say!—One; two: why, then 'tis time to do't.—Hell is murky.—Fie, my Lord, fie! a soldier and afeard?—What need we fear who knows it, when none can call our power to account?—Yet who would have thought the old man to have so much blood in him? The Thane of Fife had a wife: where is she now?—What, will these hands ne'er be clean?—No more o'that, my Lord, no more o'that: you mar all with this starting. Here's the smell of the blood still; all the perfumes of Arabia will not sweeten this little hand. Oh! oh! oh! Wash your hands, put on your night-gown; look not so pale.—I tell you again, Banquo's dead and buried: he cannot come out on's grave. To bed to bed: there's knocking at the gate. Come, come, come, come, what's done cannot be undone. To bed, to bed, to bed.

Pause

I know why she went mad, Doll. It was the waiting, the waiting.
Doll You've not gone mad, have you?
Mrs Betterton Me? No. I'm just eccentric. Old and eccentric. Come along.

She gets up slowly and exits

SCENE 8

The stage darkens. It is the nether world

Doll warms herself by the fire

Nell enters

Nell Doll, Doll. Is that you, Doll?

Pause

I must have been dreaming. Or sleeping.
Doll How was your house?
Nell Oh, you know. Lots of cushions.
Doll Oh dear.
Nell No. I liked them.
Doll Everyone said you was very happy.
Nell On the whole. We had our problems. Most couples do. Sometimes he'd go on and on about his dad. You know.
Doll Well, he would.
Nell Yeah. But it's not as if I ever met him. I told him. My mum died pissed with her head in a puddle. I don't go on about it, do I?
Doll I can see your point.
Nell He kept on and on about the blood and the slicing. You expect more off of a monarch.

Pause

I had me picture done. Stark naked. He'd sit and look at it for ages. Just him looking at me. Hours, and the room'd turn dark.

Pause

I couldn't sleep some nights. The house seemed empty.
Doll Big places do.
Nell Sometimes I'd get restless. Restless.

Pause

Still. I never did nothing I didn't want to. Did I?

Pause

Eh, Doll?

Doll You don't see nothing. Do ya? Playhouse creatures, they called you. And them was the polite ones. Like you was animals.

Nell Animals?

Doll Before this place turned playhouse it was a bear pit. They hated to dance for a whip. My dad was the bear keeper. One day this bear turned on him. The whip came down and down on her and still she came. She slashed his chest, here to here. That night they took out her claws and teeth. Ripped em out, and she howled and screamed and rocked in pain. It woke me and I ran in. There was blood on the floor. "No, dad, no," I says. And he said "You let one of them get away with it and tomorrow none of them bears'll dance". The bear had gone still and her head was hanging and I said "Why should you whip her?" He took my hand and put it in the blood that was on the floor and then he wiped more on my face. "She dances and we eat meat," he said. "Never let me hear you speak on it again." The blood was warm at first and then it started turning cold on me and it seemed to turn me cold. I never did say nothing again.

Pause

Playhouse creatures they called you like you was animals.

Nell But we spoke and we was the first!

Doll And where'd it get you?

Pause

Nell I'm going to do an epilogue. Do it with us? For old times' sake?

Doll I can't remember no epilogues. My mind's prone to wander.

Nell We'll make one up. Go on, Doll. I'm going to dedicate it to Mrs Betterton.

Doll Mrs B?

Nell Yeah.

Doll She'd have liked that.

Nell Yeah. Look around. There's no-one here, Doll. Just us. Those promises we made. They're old. Dust. Now we can say what we like.

Doll What will we say?

Nell Anything. Now we can say anything.

They come forward together as if to begin an epilogue. The Lights go down

CURTAIN

FURNITURE AND PROPERTY LIST

Further dressing may be added at the director's discretion

PROLOGUE

On stage: Small fire

ACT I

SCENE 1

On stage: As before

Personal: **Doll:** bell

SCENE 2

On stage: As before

Personal: **Nell:** jug, sixpence

SCENE 3

Set: Tree

Strike: Small fire

Off stage: Oranges (**Nell**)

Personal: **Mrs Betterton:** bows and arrows
                 Mrs Marshall: bows and arrows

Scene 4

Strike: Tree

Personal: **Doll:** bowl
              Cleopatra: 2 asps
              Charmian: asp

Scene 5

On stage: Pot

Scene 6

Set: Various items of costume

Strike: Pot

Scene 7

On stage: As before

Scene 8

Strike: Various items of costume

Personal: **Mrs Marshall:** dagger

Scene 9

Set: Various items of costume

Personal: **Mrs Marshall:** handkerchief

SCENE 10

Set:	Shawl Broomstick
Off stage:	**Doll's part (Mrs Betterton)** **Candle (Mrs Betterton)**
Personal:	**Mrs Marshall:** small knife, 3 pins **Nell:** coin

ACT II

SCENE 1

Strike:	Shawl Broomstick
Personal:	**Nell:** sword **Mrs Marshall:** sword

SCENE 2

On stage:	Costume brooch with a long pin Cloth
Personal:	**Mrs Betterton:** long piece of yarn **Lady Fanciful:** hand mirror

SCENE 3

Strike:	Costume brooch Cloth
Off stage:	Sack of props. *In it:* 3 dutch collars, spoon, crown, jerkin, eaglet, bread roll, scrap of fur, 2 beads, curtains (**Doll**)

SCENE 4

On stage: As before

SCENE 5

On stage: Various items of costume, including shawl
              Bag. *In it:* **Mrs Betterton**'s parts (papers etc.)
              Cup

Personal: **Nell:** mirror, a few belongings

SCENE 6

Strike: Various items of costume, including shawl
              Bag. *In it:* **Mrs Betterton**'s parts
              Cup

SCENE 7

On stage: **Nell**'s parts

SCENE 8

On stage: Fire

LIGHTING PLOT

Property fittings required: nil
2 interior, 1 exterior settings.

PROLOGUE

To open: Overall general lighting

No cues

ACT I, SCENE 1

To open: Overall general lighting

No cues

ACT I, SCENE 2

To open: Overall general lighting

Cue 1   **Mrs Farley** enters   (Page 3)
           Bring up bright sunshine effect

ACT I, SCENE 3

To open: General lighting

Cue 2   **Nell:** "The Fatal Maiden!"   (Page 7)
           Lights come up on Mrs Farley

ACT I, SCENE 4

To open: Overall general lighting

No cues

ACT I, SCENE 5

To open: Overall general lighting

No cues

ACT I, SCENE 6

To open: Overall general lighting

No cues

ACT I, SCENE 7

To open: Overall general lighting

No cues

ACT I, SCENE 8

To open: Overall general lighting

No cues

ACT I, SCENE 9

To open: Overall general lighting

No cues

ACT I, SCENE 10

To open: Overall general lighting

No cues

ACT II, SCENE 1

To open: Overall general lighting

No cues

ACT II, Scene 2

To open: Overall general lighting

No cues

ACT II, Scene 3

To open: Overall general lighting

No cues

ACT II, Scene 4

To open: Overall general lighting

No cues

ACT II, Scene 5

To open: Overall general lighting

Cue 3   **Doll: "The end!"**   (Page 53)
         Fade lights, bring up a brief orange glow,
            then black-out

ACT II, Scene 6

To open: Overall general lighting

No cues

ACT II, Scene 7

To open: Overall general lighting

No cues

ACT II, SCENE 8

To open: Fade lights

Cue 4   **Nell:** "Now we can say anything."   (Page 60)
         Fade lights to black-out

EFFECTS PLOT

ACT I

Cue 1   **Nell:** "It has a decent, reg'lar sort of clientele."   (Page 5)
          A bellow is heard from the Cock and Pie

Cue 2   **Mrs Marshall:** "She'd better be proficient."   (Page 19)
          Noises off stage

Cue 3   **Doll:** "There's ladies changing in here."   (Page 20)
          Noise surges

Cue 4   **Doll:** "You can wait till after and it'll cost ya."   (Page 20)
          Noise surges again

Cue 5   **Mrs Marshall:** "...ball-driven fuckwits."   (Page 20)
          Cut noise

Cue 6   **Mrs Marshall:** "Ta."   (Page 25)
          Noises off stage